Starting a New Business In Massachusetts

A Guide to Financial, Tax & Accounting Considerations of Starting a Successful Business

Agranovich Accounting and Payroll Solutions
1007 Chestnut St Suite A
Newton, MA, 02464
(617) 840-0982
(617) 845-0405 Fax
Email: lev@agstax.com
http://www.agstax.com

I0048292

ABOUT AGRANOVICH ACCOUNTING AND PAYROLL

Agranovich Accounting and Payroll Services are a full service tax preparation, payroll, accounting and business consulting firm located in Newton, MA. Our firm provides outstanding service to our clients because of our dedication to the three underlying principles of *professionalism, responsive and quality.*

Professionalism

Our firm is one of the leading firms in the area. By combining our expertise, experience and the energy of our staff, each client receives close personal and professional attention.

Our high standards, service and specialized staff spell the difference between our outstanding performance, and other firms. We make sure that every client is served by the expertise of our whole firm.

Responsiveness

Our firm is responsive. Companies who choose our firm rely on competent advice and fast, accurate personnel. We provide total financial services to individuals, large and small businesses and other agencies.

To see a listing of our services, please take a moment and look at our services page. Because we get new business from the people who know us best, client referrals have fueled our growth in the recent years.

Through hard work, we have earned the respect of the business and financial communities. This respect illustrates our diverse talents, dedication and ability to respond quickly.

Quality

An accounting firm is known for the quality of its service. Our firm's reputation reflects the high standards we demand of ourselves.

Our primary goal as a trusted advisor is to be available to provide insightful advice to enable our clients to make informed financial decisions. We do not accept anything less from ourselves and this is what we deliver to you.

We feel it is extremely important to continually professionally educate ourselves to improve our technical expertise, financial knowledge and service to our clients.

Our high service quality and "raving fan" clients are the result of our commitment to excellence.

We welcome you to contact us anytime.

Agranovich Accounting and Payroll

1007 Chestnut St. Suite A

Newton, MA, 02464

Phone: (617)840-0982

lev@agstax.com

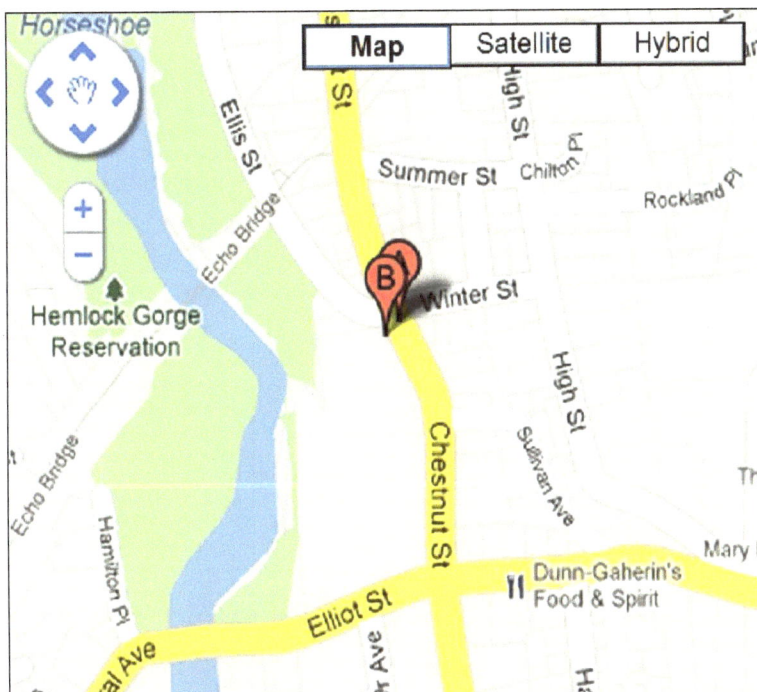

INTRODUCTION

Why do people start a small business? It is the ambition of many people to run their own business. In recent years this dream has become a reality for some who have been made **redundant**, whilst others may decide to start up in business to be more independent and to obtain the full financial reward for their efforts. Some want to spend more time with family, and starting a business allows them to do that. Some find it exhausting to be outside the house all day, dealing with traffic, co-workers, meetings and interruptions. Some people hate answering to a boss all the time- needing permission to schedule a dentist appointment or take the day off when they're sick. Some people are unmotivated by the security of a regular paycheck and prefer the challenge of the direct rewards or losses that entrepreneur see from their efforts. Becoming a business owner has unique challenges and rewards that aren't right for everyone. You must be driven, disciplined and able to identify a product or service that people need - one that they will pay enough to allow you to live comfortably. You have to develop marketing skills and be able to find your own work, because it won't fall into your lap until after you're well established. Business owners need to understand how to budget, keep records and handle small business taxes. They must familiarize themselves with employment laws if they want to hire staff. They also need a plan for protecting their business and everything that's tied to it if something goes wrong.

Whatever the reason for considering setting up **in** business, a number of dangers exist. A major concern must be the risk of business failure despite considerable effort and finance having been put into the venture. Time spent in making the decision and thinking through your plans will minimize the risk of failure. Think carefully about ceasing to be someone else's employee. Certainty of income, both in terms of quantity and regularity, disappears, whilst fixed outgoings, such as mortgage repayments, remain. Similarly, other benefits of employment may be lost, such as life assurance cover, a company pension, medical insurance, a company car, regular hours and holidays. Consider the views of your family and friends. Their support is essential. It is important they understand that the administrative and financial requirements of running a business can be time consuming and stressful. Success in business depends on many factors; most important is the need to critically review all aspects of the business proposition before progressing too far. This kit highlights many of the practical points that require consideration before trading begins.

ON YOUR WAY

Starting a business can sometimes seem like an uphill climb. You must plan each step before you take it. Once a business plan is developed, the entrepreneur must consider more than production, marketing, and accounting. You must also consider the legal environment and government regulation of business and the related forms necessary to comply with regulation. The following activities should be considered when starting a new business:

- Consult an attorney regarding the legal requirements of setting up and operating your business.

- Consult an accountant regarding the financial and tax requirements of setting up and operating your   business.

- Register the name of the business with the state.

- Make appropriate applications for licenses to operate in desired states.

- Obtain a federal employer identification number (Form SS-4).

- Apply for state workers' compensation and unemployment insurance.

- Determine applicable job safety and health regulations (OSHA).

- Determine applicable environmental regulations.

- Apply for local business licenses.

TABLE OF CONTENTS

CHAPTER 7: INCOME TAXES

CHAPTER 8: PAYROLL TAXES

CHAPTER 9:   INSURANCE

CHAPTER 10: SELECTING YOUR BUSINESS ADVISORS

CONCLUSION

CHAPTER 1

SELECTING A LEGAL ENTITY

"Creating value for customers builds loyalty, and loyalty in turns builds growth, profit, and more value."

- Frederik Reichheld

The Loyalty Effect

Choosing an Entity Type

One of the first decisions you will encounter in starting a new business is choosing a business structure. Here is an explanation of various structures and how they affect a company's tax treatment or liability. Before you enter into any one of these business structures, the Massachusetts Office of Business Development (MOBD) strongly recommends that you seek legal and accounting advice.

SOLE PROPRIETORSHIP, PARTNERSHIP, CORPORATION

The **Sole Proprietorship** is the simplest form of business. To form a sole proprietorship, you just have to let people know that you are in business and file a form in the city or town hall where you are going to do business. You personally are responsible for all debts and other legal liabilities of your business. The income from your business is reported to the IRS as part of your personal income and taxed accordingly.

A **Partnership** is formed when two or more people decide to go into business together. It is called a conduit because, though persons have banded together for a profit-producing motive, it is generally not considered a legal entity separate from the partners. Thus, a partnership may not be sued or sue in its firm name only, and each partner shares a potential joint and separate liability.

In a "general" partnership, each partner is totally liable for whatever happens to the business, and for whatever the other person does. Normally, a general partner has unlimited liability, which includes personally owned assets outside the business assets.

A "limited" partner is liable only for the amount of money he or she invests into the business, but there must be at least one general partner who is liable for the total. Income from a partnership is reported to the IRS as part of each partner's personal income and taxed accordingly.

In creating a **Corporation** you are creating a legal entity. From then on, your business has an identity of its own. It has certain rights. It can sue and be sued. It has to file its own tax returns, etc. The ownership of a corporation is divided into "stocks," which are sometimes called "shares." The owners are called "stockholders." One person can own all of the stocks, in which case there is only one stockholder. A stockholder meeting has to be held at least once a year to decide how to manage the company and what to do about profits or losses. The profits can be reinvested in the business or distributed among the stockholders as "dividends." Control and profit division is proportional to the stocks held. The person who has 51% of the stocks will have 51% of the dividends.

An **S Corporation** is a hybrid corporation that is treated like a partnership for many (but not all) tax purposes. It has virtually all of the features of a corporation, e.g., limited liability. The S corporation is treated like a partnership in those profits and losses typically are taxed directly to the individual shareholders, and it is their responsibility to report these gains or losses on their individual income tax returns.

S CORPORATION ELECTION

A corporation may elect not to be subject to the taxes imposed on regular corporations but rather pass its income, losses and deductions through to its shareholders. Qualifications of an S corporation must be met as of the first day of the first tax year of the corporation for which the election is to be effective. The election is valid only if all the shareholders in the corporation consent to the election. To qualify, a corporation must satisfy each of the following conditions:

- Must be a domestic corporation

- Must have no more than 75 shareholders

- Each shareholder must be an individual, an estate, or a specified type of trust.

- No shareholder may be a corporation or a non-resident alien.

- Can have only one class of stock. (However, different voting rights are allowable.)

If you qualify, you must file **Election Form 2553** with the Internal Revenue Service. For further information, contact Agranovich Accounting and Payroll office or call (617) 840-0982. if the company qualifies under the IRS requirements, then the Commonwealth of Massachusetts will recognize the company as an S corporation.

A CORPORATION: ISSUES TO CONSIDER

Limited Liability. If your business is a corporation, your liability is only limited to the amount of assets in your business (except in the case of a loan for which you offer your personal guaranty). Therefore, creditors and plaintiffs in lawsuits cannot make claims upon your personal assets.

Ease of Raising Capital and Transferability. Since owners of a corporation are liable only for the amount they invest, it is much easier to convince other people to invest in the business in exchange for a certain percentage of the profit. If one of the owners wants to pull out, all they have to do is find someone to buy their share of the business. If any one of the owners dies, his/her heirs

inherit that share of the business. There is no interruption in the day-to-day operation of the business.

Ease of Separating Ownership from Management. The owners (or stockholders) of a corporation may decide they don't want to run the business themselves. They can hire a professional manager to run it. If they do not like the manager, they can call a board meeting and replace that person. The line between ownership and management can be clear-cut.

Taxes. The tax rates differ for corporations and other forms of business. An accountant can recommend how you can set up your business to get the most tax advantages.

Costs. It costs $200.00 to become incorporated. This does not include lawyers' or filing fees. There are additional costs in doing business because you will be subjected to some regulations that cover corporations and not other forms of business.

NOTE: Federal Corporate Income Taxes to Shareholders - If an S Corporation designation is elected and qualifies under the required time to make such an election, the corporation will not pay corporate income taxes on income. The shareholders will pay taxes on corporate profit even though it may not be distributed.

TO INCORPORATE OR NOT

One of the myths about business is that corporations are big companies. Not necessarily true. The same person can be the president, treasurer, and clerk of the corporation. The only requirement in Massachusetts is that the person designated to be the clerk has to be a resident of the Commonwealth. The selection of the type of business is not irrevocable. Partnerships and proprietorships can usually be incorporated without tax incidence. (Regular corporations electing S corporation status or terminating corporate status and returning to partnership or proprietorship status involve substantially more complex planning. Neither of these steps should be undertaken without competent professional advice.) A corporation can elect S corporation status if it meets the eligibility requirements even after it has operated as a regular corporation for many years. Alternatively, an S corporation can terminate its special status at any time and, on a prospective basis, return to a regular corporation for tax purposes. The company will generally be required to wait five years before it can re-elect S corporation status.

LIMITED LIABILITY COMPANY AND PARTNERSHIP

Since January 1, 1996, two new types of business entities have been available in the Commonwealth: Limited Liability Companies and Limited Liability Partnerships.

A Limited Liability Company (LLC) is an unincorporated association which combines the advantage of limited liability for participants with the favorable tax treatment of a partnership. The participants, referred to as members, can participate in management control of the business without increasing their personal exposure beyond their contribution to the business.

Like corporations, LLCs are created by compliance with statute MGL c.156C, including filing a certificate of organization with the Secretary of State. The filing fee is $500. Once created, LLCs function in accordance with the terms of the operating agreement, a document comparable to a partnership agreement. LLCs must also file an annual report with the Secretary of State. This filing fee is also $500.

A limited liability partnership (LLP) is a partnership which, by registering with the Secretary of State, limits the personal liability of a partner for debts, obligations, and liabilities of the partnership, whether in tort, contract or otherwise from negligence, wrongful acts, errors or omissions, except that a partner cannot eliminate liability for his own negligence. The filing fee for registration is $500. LLPs must also file an annual report with the Secretary of State (also $500).

CHAPTER 2

BUILDING UP A BUSINESS PLAN

"You get out of life what you put into it ... it's the same with business. A clear and impactful plan makes a massive difference to achieving this. With a great plan you can engage others with a sense of direction and purpose align all activities and review progress"

\- Matthew Brearley

BUILDING UP A BUSINESS PLAN

Why do I need a written Business Plan?

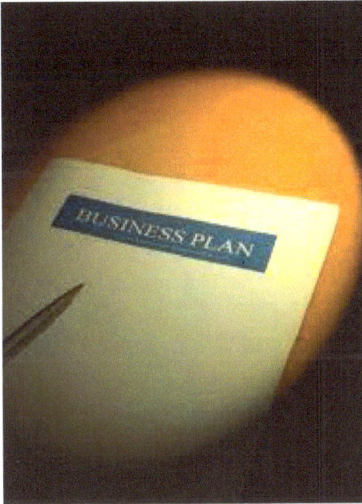

Financial aiding is the only use many people perceive for a written business plan. However, if you are just starting a business, a written plan may also serve as a "blueprint" to facilitate you organize and consider out all of their aspects of your future business. While many entrepreneurs begin with only an informal plan for their operations, note down the plan will ensure that nothing "slips through the cracks" in the planning process. It will also serve as means to measure the success and progress of your business.

Requirements to incorporate in my plan

The quality of your product/service is important to your brand because it is the core value that your customers expect. A high quality product/service is fundamental for success as a new business. When your product/service exceeds your customers' expectations, they tend to associate their positive experiences with your brand, are more likely to use your product/service again, and share it with others.

a) ACCOUNTANT

Your accountant should be a practical business advisor who can set up a total financial-control system for your business and render sound business advice. At the outset, your accountant should work with you to establish accounting and reporting systems, cash projections, financing strategies and tax planning. In addition, as the company matures, the following services can be provided:

- Strategic planning.

- Your choice of business type.

- Cash-management advice.

- Merger, acquisition and appraisal assistance.

- Compensation strategies.

- Cost-reduction planning.

- Management information systems.

b) INSURANCE

Most businesses require insurance in one form or another. Some forms, such as workers' compensation, may be required by law. Others, such as liability insurance, may not be required by law but should be purchased by most businesses.

The entrepreneur should shop around to find the insurer who offers the best combination of coverage, service and price. Trade associations often offer special rates and policies to their members.

Below is a list of insurance coverage you should consider:

- Workers' Compensation - (Mandatory)

- Automobile Insurance - (Mandatory)

- Liability Insurance - Protecting the business from claims of bodily injury, property damage, and malpractice.

- Fire Insurance

- Business Interruption Insurance-Compensating the business for revenue lost during a temporary halt of business caused by fire, theft, or illness.

- Crime Coverage - Reimbursing the employer for robbery, burglary, and vandalism losses.

- Group Life Insurance - (for employer and employees)

- Disability Insurance - (for employer and employees)

- Key-Person Insurance - Compensating business for the death or disability of a key partner of manager.

- Fidelity Bonds - Insuring the employer from employee theft.

- Product Liability Insurance

c) ATTORNEY

Laws and legal requirements enter into most aspects of business and can vary greatly from state to state. An attorney should be consulted to help you meet many of the legal requirements facing you and your business, including:

- Employee relations.

- Partnership agreements.

- Obtaining licenses.

- Reviewing and negotiating contracts.

- Reviewing various laws and regulations.

- Antitrust, product liability, and environmental concerns.

- Protection of your idea or product.

CHAPTER 3

BRANDING YOUR BUSINESS

"Everything should be made as simple as possible, but not simpler."

- Albert Einstein

BRANDING YOUR BUSINESS

Before You Choose a Name

When choosing a name for your business you might want to begin by looking at types of names that are already being used by businesses similar to your own. There are several sources of such information. You can find lists of business names at the Corporations Division of the Secretary of State, your local city or town hall, in the library, in relevant trade journals, and even in the telephone book.

As you are considering possible names you must take care to choose a name that is not already being used by another business. Do everything you can within reason to assure that yours will be the only business of that type using a particular name.

If you decide to incorporate your business, you must contact Agranovich Accounting and Payroll Services. If you have decided on a name for your corporation but are not yet ready to incorporate, you can reserve a name for 30 days. This reservation will protect the business name from infringement while you prepare to incorporate and should be done before taking any other steps to do business in the state. A corporate name may not be reserved by a telephone request. The reservation of a name for 60 days becomes effective only upon written request to the Corporations Division and payment of a $30 fee.

For further information contact

Agranovich Accounting and Payroll
1007 Chestnut St. Suite A
Newton, MA, 02464
Phone: (617)840-0982
lev@agstax.com

You will be prohibited from using a name if another corporation is already using it or one that is very similar. An exemption may be made if you are able to obtain a letter of consent from the other corporation giving you permission to use a similar name.

Choosing a Name

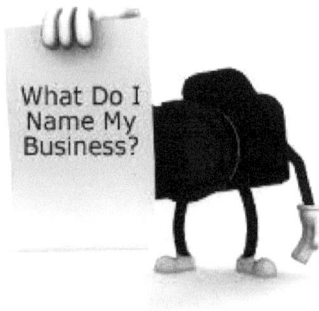

Choosing a baby's name is one of the first and most significant decisions that any new parents must make. The same can be said for the decision facing you, the new "parent" of a brand new business. Your business name is one of your most important business assets and should be chosen carefully. The following information describes three types of business names, outlines the research you should do before choosing a name, and defines filing requirements as well as how to register a service mark or a trademark.

What is the difference between a trade name and a trademark? Before you select your business name you need to understand how the kinds of business names differ. Names fall into three categories:

  a. **Trade Name** identifies a company, e.g., the "Coca Cola Company" or "Computer Services." Any type of business may call itself a company.

  b. **Corporate Names** identify corporations, e.g., "Cabot Corporation" or "Marketing Concepts, Inc." The words "Incorporated," "Corporation," or "limited," or their abbreviations, must appear in a corporate name and may not appear in the name of an unincorporated company.

  c. **Trademarks** are any word, name, symbol, or device or any combination of these used to identify the goods of a business and distinguish those goods from the products of others. For example, the word "Kleenex" is a trademark.

Similarly, there are **service marks** which may be used to identify and distinguish a business that provides a service rather than goods. For example, the word "Greyhound" is a service mark for transportation services.

Business Obligations

- Required Filings After Your Name is Chosen

- Corporation - Articles of Organization - Secretary of State's Office

- Limited Liability Partnership - A Certificate of Lt. Liability Partnership - Secretary of State's Office

- Limited Liability Corporation - A Certificate of Lt. Liability Corporation - Secretary of State's Office

- General Partnership - Doing Business As (dba) Certificate Local City or Town Hall

- Sole Proprietorship dba Certification Local City or Town Hall

What you must do after you have a name for your business is largely determined by the type of business you have set up. Use the following chart as a check list to determine (1) whether you must file organizational forms with the state, and (2) whether you must file a business certificate in your local community. Remember that many businesses are regulated and that you may need to apply for state and/or local permits or licenses before you begin. Since laws, regulations, rulings, and rates continually change, your lawyer and accountant should be contacted.

Local Filing

Under Massachusetts law, a person doing business under a name different than his/her own must file a business certificate, or "dba" (doing business as), at the city or town hall clerk's office where you maintain an office. If the company has

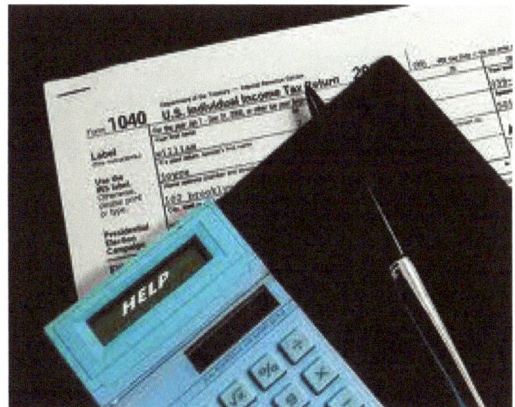

more than one location, you must register in the city or town where the headquarters are located. The fee for this filing varies from town to town but is approximately $25 for four years. The only case in which you do not have to file a "dba" is when you are doing business as a sole proprietor under your own complete name, such as "John Smith Company." Your filing of a business certificate at the local level does not protect your name as does a corporate filing or a trademark registration. A business certificate primarily allows consumers and creditors to identify the names of the actual owners of a business. Therefore, a city or town clerk may even accept more than one certificate with an identical business name in order to provide this public record.

Filing Name and Purpose of Corporation

There can be as few as one person to establish a corporation. You must state the purpose of the corporation. Taxes and liability considerations should determine business forms. The filing fee is $200, which enables corporations to issue stock. You do not have to file with your city or town hall if you file with the Secretary of State's Office.

For further information contact

Agranovich Accounting and Payroll

Phone: (617)840-0982

lev@agstax.com

Trademark and Service Mark

Whether you are just starting out in business or have been in business for a number of years, you should consider protecting your right to any trademarks or service marks you may own. The quality and goodwill symbolized by a distinctive mark can be a very valuable commodity to a business and one worthy of protection from infringement. Non-profit organizations also have an interest in protecting their distinctive marks from unwanted infringement.

- **Trademark** is any word, name, symbol, or device, or any combination of these, used by a person (that is, an individual, a firm or partnership, a corporation, or any type of association) to distinguish his or her goods from others. Some examples of well-known trademarks are: Kodak, Coca-Cola, GE, Lifesavers, and the banana lady on a bunch of Chiquita Bananas.

- **Service Mark** identifies and distinguishes a person's services and is given the same protection as a trademark. Some examples of well-known service marks are: Rock of Gibraltar - Prudential Insurance Company; Greyhound Bus Lines' Greyhound; and the Golden Arches of McDonald's.

Under the terms of the trademark law there is no requirement that a trademark or service mark must be registered with the Commonwealth of Massachusetts.

How to Register a Mark

A mark must be in use in Massachusetts before it may be registered. A mark may then be registered by completing the appropriate trademark or service mark registration application form. The fee for filing is $50 and the effective term of the registration is ten years, and the mark may be renewed every ten years.

Registration of a mark in Massachusetts results in material advantages to the owner of a mark. A central card file is made available for public inspection in the Trademarks Division office. A person who might have otherwise used a mark identical or confusingly similar to a registered mark may discover the prior use of the mark in a preliminary search of these files. This early warning could mean such a person would use a different mark and a possible controversy may be prevented.

There are evidentiary benefits, as well, that accrue to the registrant of a mark. The Certificate of Registration issued by the Division creates certain presumptions of exclusive ownership of the mark by the registrant which are of significant benefit to the registrant in any type of dispute over his mark.

These application forms as well as further information regarding trademarks or service marks may be obtained by contacting:

Agranovich Accounting and Payroll

Phone: (617)840-0982

lev@agstax.com

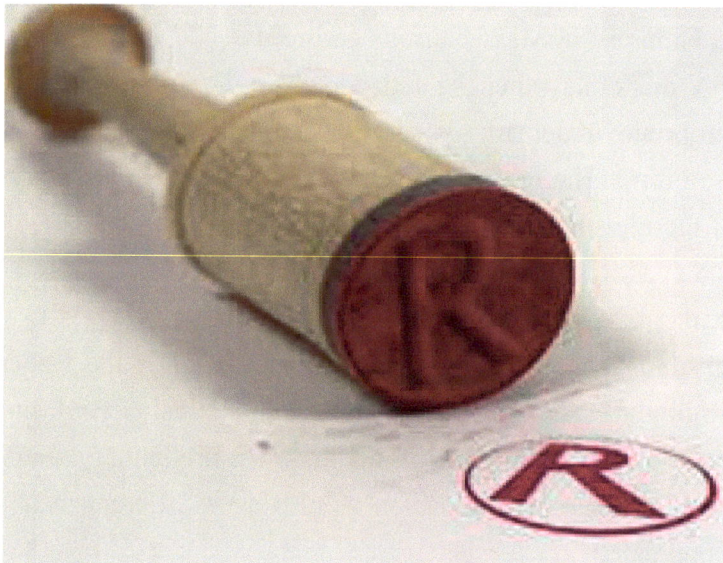

CHAPTER 4

TAX PLANNING

"In this world nothing can be said to be certain, except death and taxes."
- Benjamin Franlin

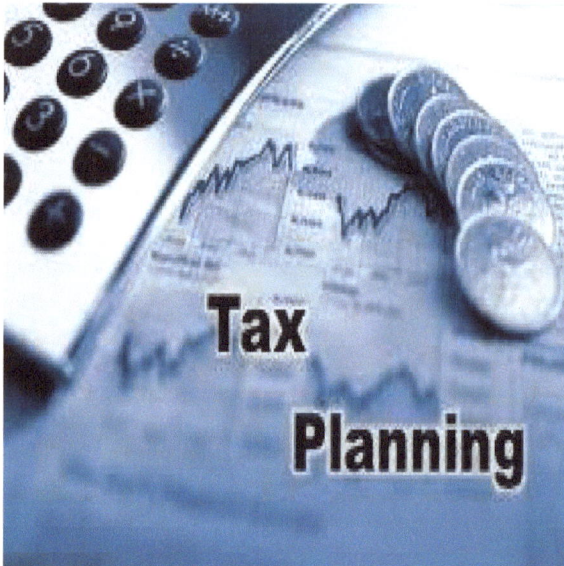

Crunching the Numbers

When you begin your business, you must consider what tax year to use. The term "tax year" means your annual accounting period, calendar year or fiscal year period of no more than 12 months, except in the case of a 52/53 week tax year. The 52/53 week allows taxpayers to close the tax year on the same day of the week every year (e.g., last Saturday in December). Each business form has its own requirements regarding which accounting period to choose. Corporations, other than personal-service corporations, may choose any year-end.

Personal service corporations, partnerships and S corporations are generally limited to a calendar year. Generally, they may elect a different tax year only if such tax year results in a deferral not longer than three months. In the case of electing partnership or S corporation, the partnership or S corporation must make certain required tax payments. An electing personal-service corporation is required to meet minimum distribution requirements in the deferral period. Usually, sole proprietors use the calendar year.

One of the most important items to consider in choosing a year-end, however, is your business season (or natural business year). You may want to end the year during your slow season to make the year-end closing period easier.

This section discusses some of the more important options minimizing current and future income tax liabilities.

Cash Conservation through Tax Planning

Deferring income taxes to be paid in the future can have a significant impact on the capital needs of a growing business. Deferring taxes is essentially an "interest-free" loan from the government, freeing up cash that would otherwise have to be borrowed to finance inventories or capital expansion.

A profitable business is not the only entity that can benefit from tax planning. In start-up ventures conducted in a "flow-through" entity form (proprietorship, S corporation or partnership), good tax planning can minimize the losses currently deductible by entrepreneurs/partners/shareholders, enabling them to increase the amount of their capital available to the business. Furthermore, as seen in the following discussions, much of the groundwork for good future tax planning is established in a venture's first year.

For further information contact

Agranovich Accounting and Payroll

1007 Chestnut St. Suite A

Newton, MA, 02464

Phone: (617)840-0982

lev@agstax.com

CHAPTER 5

ACCOUNTING METHODS

"There is no business like show business. But there are several like accounting."

- David Letterman

ACCOUNTING METHODS

Cash Method is the most common overall methods used to compute income are the cash receipts-and-disbursement method and the accrual method. In most cases, a company will elect a method of accounting in its tax return that provides immediate tax benefits. The cash method, which recognizes income and expense based on when cash is received and disbursed, provides the most flexible means of differing taxable income into future tax years. Use of the cash method is restricted, however. Corporations with average annual gross receipts, during the specified base period, of more than $5 million must use the accrual or another IRS-approved method of tax accounting. Partnerships (if they have no regular corporations as partners) and S corporations that are not tax shelters may continue to use the cash method regardless of their gross receipts. The cash method generally cannot be used if inventories are a significant portion of a company's business.

Accrual Method recognizes income and expenses based on when income is earned or an obligation to pay a debt is incurred, generally provides better matching of revenue and expenditures. This method is typically required for financial reporting purposes. For tax purposes, the taxpayer must compute taxable income under the method of accounting regularly used to compute income in keeping books (regardless of the method used for financial reporting) unless the method used does not clearly reflect income.

Once a method of accounting is adopted it can be changed only with IRS permission. Permission is usually granted in the case of switching from the cash method to the accrual method; it is routinely denied in switching from the accrual to the cash method.

Cash and accrual methods are overall accounting methods of the business. In addition to on overall method, more specialized accounting methods are necessary for most businesses. A brief overview of these methods follows. Your tax advisor or accountant should be consulted for further details.

Inventory Methods

In the first year in which the business has inventory, it must choose an appropriate method to account for that inventory. Methods commonly used are *average cost; first-in, first-out (FIFO); and last-in, first-out (LIFO) methods.*

- **Average Cost Method.** This method prices inventory on the basis of the average cost of all similar goods available during the period. It is mainly used because it is simple and relatively easy to use.

- **First-In, First-Out (FIFO) Method.** This method assumes that inventory is used in the order that it is purchased or produced. Under this method, ending inventory is stated at approximate current costs, with the oldest cost charged against current sales. In periods of inflation, this can cause "paper profits" to be recognized and taxed. It also results in the highest reported earnings. The FIFO method is probably the most commonly used inventory control.

- **Last-In, First-Out (LIFO) Method**. This method became popular in prior years due to significant inflation. The LIFO method assumed that the most recently purchased or produced goods are used first - the opposite assumption from FIFO. Although generally this is a more difficult method to use, a simplified LIFO method of accounting of inventories is available to small business. A taxpayer can use the simplified LIFO method if average annual gross receipts for the three proceeding tax years do not exceed $5 million. In periods of inflation, LIFO results in lower inventory valuations, higher cost of sales and lower taxable income. This method is most commonly used by companies facing rising production and material costs. The LIFO inventory method is adopted by filing Form 970 with the income tax return for the tax year in which the method is first used.

Overhead Costs

A mechanism must be established to capture overhead costs and relate them to an inventory's direct material and labor costs. Manufacturers typically allocate the "poll" of indirect costs to inventory on the basis of a standard unit, such as labor dollars or hours. Once a method has been established, it cannot be changed without IRS permission. As a result,

many of the planning techniques for inventory overhead costs need to be addressed when the business is starting.

Research and Development Expenditures

Current Expense v. Amortization - Research and Development (R&D) expenses are those **expenses** incurred in developing new products, processes, etc., and expenses incurred in significantly improving existing products. There are two tax methods available for deducting R&D expenses -deduct currently or amortize over 60 months. In most cases, currently deducting provides the best answer. Once an election has been made to defer R&D expenses, that method must be continued unless IRS permission to change is received.

Long-Term Contract Methods

Taxpayers involved in the construction of property that spans a tax year-end, or in the manufacture of "unique" items not normally carried in inventory, have several specialized accounting methods available to them. The adoption of these methods allows for tax deferral potential.

- **Percentage-of-Completion Method (PCM).** A common method of accounting for long-term contracts is the percentage-of-completion method, which is typically used for financial reporting purposes. PCM recognizes income on the basis of percentage of the job that is complete based on cost incurred. This method "smoothed out" revenue earned over a number of periods and results in little, if any, deferral of income for tax purposes.

- **Percentage-of-Completion/Capitalized-Cost Method.** As instituted by the Tax Reform Act of 1986, and subsequently modified by the Revenue Act of 1987, this method replaces the completed-contract method of accounting. The new method requires the taxpayers to use PCM for 70% of the contract. The balance of the contract is reported according to the taxpayer's regular method of accounting (e.g., completed contract).

For further information contact

Agranovich Accounting and Payroll

1007 Chestnut St. Suite A

Newton, MA, 02464

Phone: (617)840-0982

lev@agstax.com

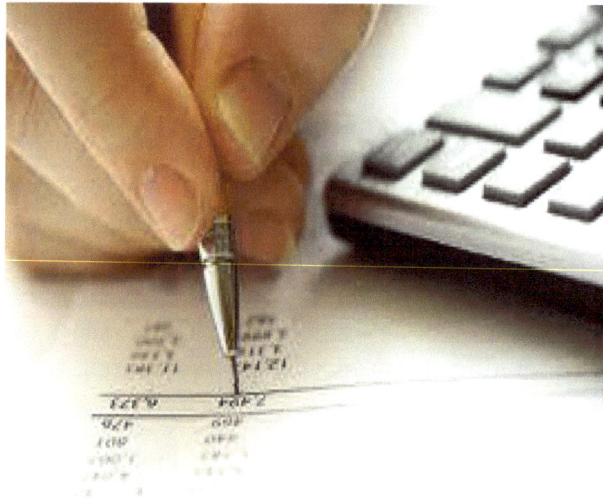

CHAPTER 6

FINANCING YOUR BUSINESS

"Wealth consists not in having great possessions, but in having few wants."

- Epictetus

Preparing for Financing

You do not need a business plan or outside consultants to know that every business needs money to operate. However, the amount needed and the time period for which the funds are required may vary for many reasons. Plan ahead and do not let your financial requirements surprise you. Arranging financing takes time and rushing decisions can be costly.

What Do You Need to Know

Before you set out to secure financing for your business you must develop a business plan or financing proposal. This proposal will represent your business to potential investors. The following is a list of information that should be included in a financing proposal:

- Information about your proposed market-Who your customer will be; why they will buy from you; how you are going to attract them.

- Information about the operation -Location, hours, staffing.

- Information about yourself-What qualifies you to run the business? (a resume should help); What is your personal financial situation?

- A list of start-up costs - It will help if you have quotes from vendors or suppliers for major equipment.

- Reasons why you need financing - How are you going to use the money; for how long; how will the funds be repaid; will you use your debt or equity.

- A beginning balance sheet- Showing what you will own (assets); what you will owe (liabilities); and what is the balance (net worth) of the first day of business assuming that financing is approved.

- A pro forma cash-flow statement-Showing how much cash you expect to flow into the business and how much cash you expect to flow out of the business, and for what reasons, for each of the next 12 months. Some financiers may ask for a projection of two years.

- A pro forma income statement- Showing how much profit you expect to make at the end of the year. (This is calculated by subtracting all the expenses from sales.) Again, you may be asked for a two year projection.

- If you are buying a business, you will need the income statement of the business for the last few years, information on why it is being sold, and why you will be able to make it profitable.

- Information on your business plan 12 and 24 months from now.

A good financial proposal takes time, research, and thoughtful consideration. You probably want to consult an accountant to check over your figures before you submit the proposal. The proposal will be judged according to the soundness of the business idea, whether the projections are realistic, and whether it is in line with the investment philosophy of the banker or organization. A judgment is also made on whether the reader is confident in your ability as an entrepreneur.

For help in developing a business plan, visit the Massachusetts Small Business Development Center Network at www.msbdc.org. The organization coordinates a network of offices across the state that provide one-to-one free comprehensive and confidential services focusing on, business growth and strategies, financing and loan assistance as well as strategic, marketing and operational analysis. See the section below for more information.

Projecting Your Cash Needs

A cash flow projection help estimate how much and for how long financing is needed. You want to borrow only the amount required and for a reasonable period. The goal is to keep interest expense as low as possible. For example, you do not want to finance short-term needs with long-term debt.

Using the projections, you can also determine when and how to repay your loans or, where an equity investment is used, estimate the amount and timing of dividend payments to investors.

Additionally, your projections can help identify when idle funds could be temporarily invested.

Sources of Capital and Financing

- **Internal**. Funds can be obtained by accelerating collection of accounts receivable, controlling expenses, leasing instead of purchasing equipment, disposing of an unprofitable product line and properly planning for federal and state taxes.

- **External**. Financing may be obtained through debt or equity financing. Each potential source has certain criteria for providing financing. Your ability to obtain financing depends on a number of factors, including: your management team, collateral, cash flow, earnings capacity and the marketability of the product.

- **Family, Friends, and Personal Savings**. In the earliest stages of development, traditional or venture capital financing is frequently not available to a new business. During this period, financing assistance from family, friends, and personal savings is often necessary to bridge the gap until you are in a position to draw on other sources of capital. Later, when you need to seek funds from prospective investors, they will take a favorable view of situations where you, as an entrepreneur, have committed a substantial portion of your personal wealth to the venture.

- **Other Sources**. Other sources of debt financing that would provide a more likely avenue for a new venture would include personal loans, loans through finance institutions to riskier and newer companies that a commercial bank might not consider (usually with a high interest rate), credit unions (for small amounts,) re-mortgaging your home, loans against life insurance, pledges or selling of notes, or contracts and bills of lading or accounts receivable (factoring), loans against inventory and credit cards. Sale-leasebacks can be a source of funds for equipment acquisitions.

- **Banks**. While new ventures generally are considered too risky to secure capital from a traditional lending institution, some banks are increasing their commitment to new business ventures. In most cases, banks will provide significant funding only after a company moves beyond the development stage. Some banks, however, are willing to lend to small businesses to finance fixed assets, inventories and accounts receivable. Where substantial collateral is available - including personal guarantees - a bank's risk declines and its willingness to make loans rises.

Massachusetts has a program that has been designed to ease small business owner's access to bank funds. It's called the Capital Access Program (CAP). $5 million has been committed by the Commonwealth of Massachusetts to provide "cash collateral" guarantees to banks willing to make loons to smaller businesses.

Here's how it works:

- The Borrower applies to a participating bank

- Bank and borrower negotiate all loan terms including pricing and guaranty premiums.

- Bank commits and funds loan using its own documentation.

- Bank notifies Massachusetts Business Development Corporation, who then provides the "cash collateral" guaranty to the bank.

For more information on the Capitol Access Program and for a list of participating banks, please contact:

Agranovich Accounting and Payroll
1007 Chestnut St. Suite A
Newton, MA, 02464
Phone: (617)840-0982
lev@agstax.com

If you are starting up a new company, you should not immediately dismiss banks as a potential lending source. Take the time to visit the banks in your area. Many banks have venture capital subsidiaries that operate in essentially the same manner as private venture capital firms. So if you fail to get a loan through traditional bank channels, a bank's venture capital firm might agree to back your company.

Private or Exempt Public Offerings. Where the amount of an offering is small and the number of investments is limited, a small growing business may be able to raise capital without fully registering with the Securities and Exchange Commission or similar state commissions. While this is unlikely to be an attractive source of financing for a start-up venture, it may be of interest to a company in an expansion phase. The entrepreneur should review with consultants the appropriateness of this financing source, considering such factors of money costs, the time lag between initiation and actual financing, the amount of financing required and the complexities introduced by having private shareholders.

Registered Public Offerings. Full-scale registration with the SEC and the state authorities is required when the amount of financing or the number of investors involved exceeds certain limits. The SEC registration requirements for small public offerings are not as stringent, but since some state lows are more restrictive, these relaxed requirements may have little significance. As with private placements, most small ventures will not view public offerings as an attractive financing source due to the time, cost and registration requirements involved, including substantial accounting and financial statement information and the acceptance of ongoing obligations of outside shareholders. Legal and accounting consultation is, of course, imperative.

For a database of financial resources available in Massachusetts, click here. (link to wherever our financial resources database is).

EQUITY

- **Partners**. Equity financing can be obtained by forming a partnership or by taking in additional general or limited partners.

- **Incorporation**. Another decision might be to incorporate and issue (or, if you are already incorporated, issue additional) common or preferred stock, convertible debt or debt with warrants attached. Your issue could be privately placed or you could go public. Venture capital could possibly be obtained, depending on the stage of your firm's life and the industry.

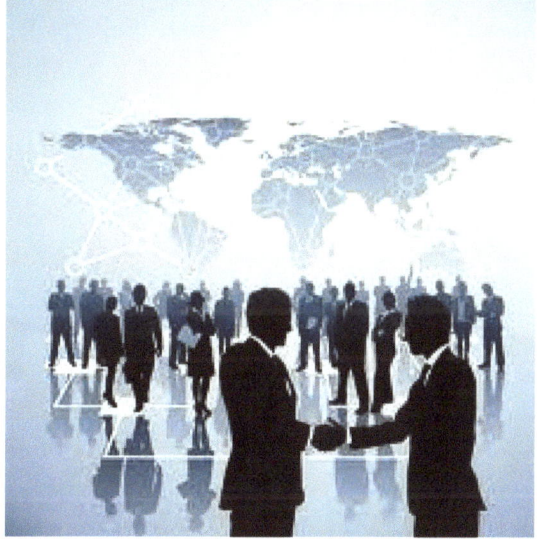

Briefly, common stock pays dividends according to profits, whereas preferred stock generally pays only a fixed amount each year. Convertible debt is debt that can be converted into common or preferred stock. Warrants enable the holder to buy shares of stock at predetermined prices. Private placements are made to a limited number of investors, as opposed to a public offering, which is made to the general investing public. Generally, venture capital is provided by sophisticated investors willing to undertake high risk on the chance that the payoff will be very large.

FEDERAL FUNDING

The U.S. Small Business Administration (SBA) provides financing to small businesses through guaranteed loans made by private lending institutions. Contact any commercial bank for more information.

- **The SBA 504 Program** uses local development companies to provide long-term financing for fixed assets with a useful life greater than 15 years. For further information contact the Agranovich Accounting and Payroll.

- **Small Business Innovation Research (SBIR) Grants** were created as part of the federal Small Business Development Act of 1982. Coordinated by the SBA, the SBIR program is designed to fund research and develop efforts which will result in bringing new products and services to the marketplace. An SBIR grant provides "idea" money for would-be entrepreneurs to use as seed capital in business start-up and for innovative science and technology-based companies to use in bringing new ventures to commercialization. By leveraging this government-funded "risk" research with private-sector financing, the SBIR program not only converts new innovations into useful products and services but also creates new business and jobs in the process. The goal of the Act is to stimulate technical innovation and encourage small scientific and high-technology companies to participate in government-funded research. The Act also provides funds for converting the results of research into commercial applications.

In order to qualify for SBIR grants, companies must conform to the federal government's definition of a small business at the time of the award. According to the program's criteria, a small business must be:

a) A U.S. corporation.

b) Independently owned and operated with 500 or fewer employees.

c) A for-profit publicly or privately held corporation, sole proprietorship, or partnership.

d) The primary source of employment for the principal investigator during the grant period.

These rules do not require that the business be established at the time a research proposal is submitted. The applicant can be employed by another company and start a new business upon receiving an SBIR grant. Also, two or more companies can enter into a joint venture, provided they qualify under the above criteria.

Under the Act, all federal agencies with research and development budgets in excess of $100 million are required to award a portion of those funds to small business through an SBIR grant program. Eleven federal agencies are now required to set aside portions of their R&D budgets under the program. They are:

a) National Association of State Development Agencies

b) National Science Foundation

c) Nuclear Regulatory Commission

d) Environmental Protection Agency

e) U.S. Department of Transportation

f) U.S. Department of Health and Human Services

g) U.S. Department of Defense

h) U.S. Department of Education

i) U.S. Department of Energy

j) U.S. Department of Agriculture

k) U.S. Department of Commerce

- **The Research and Development Limited Partnership**. This creation of the federal income tax laws has been used by both new companies and established businesses to finance research and development costs related to specific products. Because of tax law changes, R&D limited partnerships have gone through a transformation during the past few years. They used to be private placements with significant leverage. Now they are public funds without leverage and a broad portfolio of projects that are more similar to venture capital funds than anything else.

In this type of partnership, limited partners invest a specific sum that is managed by one or more general partners. The partnership then contracts with the entrepreneur to conduct research and development in exchange for certain ownership rights in the results of the R&D work. The entrepreneur retains a right to buy back the end product of this work. Because RED expenditures are currently deductible, the partners share in deductions in amounts equaling up to 80 or 90 percent of their investment in the year the R&D expenditures are incurred. However, as with other tax-favored investments, the "passive loss limits" and other provisions of the Tax Reform Act of 1986 may serve to limit or eliminate the deductibility of losses flowing from an R&D partnership and thus reduce the after-tax rate of return on the investment. If the R&D work proves successful, the entrepreneur will exercise the right to buy back the technology, generally in exchange for a percentage royalty payment based on future sales.

even project-oriented research in the right situations. There are risks, however, caused in part by the complex structure involved and by the fact that tax law in this area is still developing. Accordingly, consideration of an R&D limited partnership will necessarily require the careful and continuing involvement of an attorney and accountant.

Further, the majorities of R&D limited partnerships meet the definition of a tax shelter and may be required to be registered with the IRS as such.

VENTURE CAPITALISTS

Venture capital firms are generally privately owned. In most cases, they seek to generate a high rate of return by investing in rapidly growing businesses in all stages of development. Venture capital firms may be formed as general or limited partnerships composed primarily of institutional investors or wealthy individuals, Small Business Investment Corporations licensed by the federal government, subsidiaries or divisions of major corporations or lending institutions.

Most venture capital firms will seek investment where they expect to make a high rate of return - often 10:1 or higher - in order to maintain an annual rate of portfolio return of at least 30%. Since most new ventures fail, these high rates of return are required to offset the risk the venture capitalist assumes.

CHAPTER 7

INCOME TAXES

"Taxes are paid in the sweat of every man who labors."

- Franklin D. Roosevelt

INCOME TAXES

Tax Deductions of Property

A limited number of taxpayers are permitted to expense currently up to $10,000 of asset additions in a given year. The deduction is phased out, dollar for dollar, for any taxpayer with more than $20,000 of additions a year.

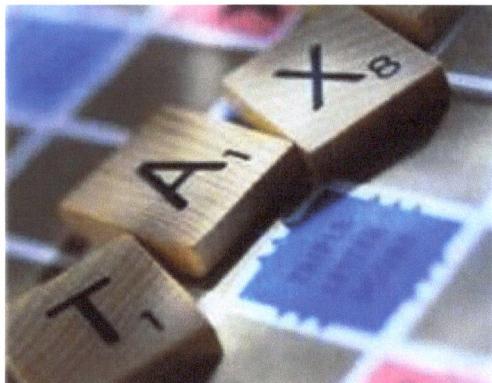

Organizational Expenses

A corporation may elect to amortize organizational expenditures over a period of not less than 60 months, beginning with the month in which the company begins business. Organizational expenditures are defined as those incidentals to the creation of the corporation, e.g., incorporation fees, legal fees, and franchise fees. The election to amortize these expenditures must be made in the company's first tax year by inclusion of statement; otherwise, the amount is deductible only in the year of dissolution. A similar election is available for partnerships, but no such election is available for sole proprietorships.

Start-up Expenses

Start-up costs are defined as costs incurred after the decision to acquire or establish a particular business but before its actual operation. These expenses are generally those that would be deducted currently if they have been incurred after the commencement of the company's operation. Start-up expenses do not include interest, taxes and research, and experimental expenses. In general, taxpayers are allowed to treat start-up costs as deferred expenses amortized over 60 months. An election to amortize must be attached to the initial return.

Modified Accelerated Cost Recovery System

Under the Modified Accelerated Cost Recovery System (MACRS) of tax depreciation, specified "cost recovery" allowances are provided for different property classes. The Tax Reform Act of 1986 created eight primary classes of property ranging from 3 to 3 1/2 year lives. For each class of property, published tables specify the percentage of the purchase price deductible as depreciation in any year.

Even though tables exist to mechanically compute annual depreciation deductions, there is still a great deal of flexibility in planning the timing and amount of depreciation deductions. For example, the straight line method (rather than the accelerated method built into the tables) can be used, if desired, over other specified extended lives. This may also be important when the business is operating in a state where net operating loss carry-overs are not allowed. It is not necessary to confirm the method of depreciation used for financial reporting purposes to the MACRS system.

Business Obligations

Once you start your business, you will have to start paying taxes to both the federal government and the Commonwealth of Massachusetts. The specific taxes you are required to pay depend on your type of business. The information in this section will help you navigate the sometimes confusing process of determining which taxes you must pay and what your filing requirements are.

Federal Identification Number

If your business is a partnership or corporation (with or without employees), or a sole proprietorship with employees, the first thing you must do is obtain a federal identification number for federal and Massachusetts tax purposes.

To obtain a federal identification number, you must file Form SS-4, Application for Employer Identification Number, with the Internal Revenue Service. This form can be downloaded from the IRS Web site, www.irs.gov, or you can have Form SS-4 sent to you by calling the IRS at (800) 829-1040. Businesses based in Massachusetts, Connecticut, Maine, New Hampshire, Rhode Island, Vermont, and New York, may fax a completed SS-4 to the IRS at (631) 447-8960, or obtain a federal identification number over the phone by calling (800) 829-4933.

Note: Sole proprietorships without employees (other than the owner), and which are not required to file excise, alcohol, tobacco, firearms do not need to obtain a federal employer identification number. They can use their Social Security number for business tax purposes.

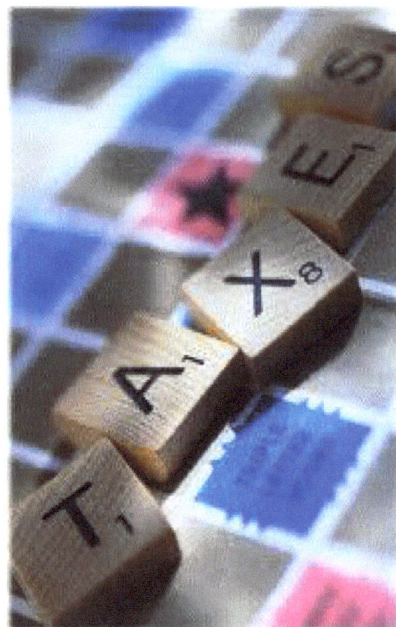

State Trustee Taxes

Trustee taxes are taxes that are collected and remitted by a business on behalf of the individuals who actually pay the taxes. In essence, the organization collecting and remitting the tax is serving as a trustee or agent. Sales, meals, withholding, and room occupancy taxes are state trustee taxes. There are also certain excise taxes you may be required to pay. You are required to register with the Massachusetts Department of Revenue for one or more of these taxes if you:

- Have people working for you in Massachusetts;

- Withhold from a pension or annuity plan or from retirement distributions;

- Sell, lease or rent taxable items in Massachusetts;

- Sell taxable telecommunications services in Massachusetts;

- Serve meals and/or beverages in Massachusetts;

- Provide lodgings in Massachusetts subject to the room occupancy excise;

- Make regular or frequent out-of-state purchases on which a use tax must be paid;

- Seek exemption from the Massachusetts sales and use tax as a charitable, nonprofit or governmental organization;

- Are licensed by any city or town in Massachusetts to sell alcoholic beverages and are organized under Chapter 180 of Massachusetts General Laws;

- Collect any of the convention center financing surcharges; or

- Sell, acquire or import cigars and/or smoking tobacco or hold cigars or smoking tobacco for sale or consumption in Massachusetts.

For additional details on trustee tax filing requirements and assistance in determining which taxes apply to your business, please contact

Agranovich Accounting and Payroll

1007 Chestnut St. Suite A

Newton, MA, 02464

Phone: (617)840-0982

lev@agstax.com

State and Federal Business Income Tax Return

Businesses and their owners are required to pay tax on business income. The type of tax they pay and the forms they file depend on how the business is organized. The tables below summarize your federal and state filing requirements. For additional detail, please consult a tax attorney, CPA or the resources listed at the end of this guide.

Sole Proprietors	State Form to File	Federal Form to File
Quarterly estimated payments Due April 15, June 15, September 15 and January 15 of the following year.	**Form 1-ES** If you expect to owe more than $400 in state tax	**Form 1040 ES** If you expect to owe more than

		Federal
		$1,000 in federal tax

Annual personal income tax return
Due 15th day of fourth month following taxable year, calendar or fiscal. If you file on a calendar-year basis, your return is due April 15.

Form 1 or Form 1 NR/PY   **Form 1040**

Profit and loss from business or profession
Due with annual state and federal personal income tax returns

Massachusetts Schedule C or a copy of federal Schedule C if no changes; or Schedule F

Schedule C (Or Schedule F for farm income)

Depreciation (if applicable)
Due with annual state and federal personal income tax returns

Copy of federal Form 4562   **Form 4562**

Self employment tax
Due with annual federal personal income tax return

N/A   **Schedule SE**

Partnerships	State Form to File	Federal Form to File
Return is due annually, by 15th day of the fourth month after the close of the partnership's taxable year, calendar or fiscal. Partnership must also issue Schedules 3K-1 to individual partners, and send copies of Schedules 3K-1 to the Department of Revenue. Partnerships have the option of sending these copies to the Department of Revenue electronically. For further information contact	**Form 3 & Schedules 3K-1 Form 1040 ES**	**Form 1065 or 1065B & Schedules K-1**

Agranovich Accounting and Payroll
1007 Chestnut St. Suite A

Newton, MA, 02464

Phone: (617)840-0982

lev@agstax.com

The following table shows which return each type of individual partner should use to report Schedule 3K-1 income:

Type of Partner	Form to File
Full-year resident individual	Form 1
Nonresident/part-year resident individual	Form 1-NR/PY
Trust or estate	Form 2
Domestic corporation	Form 355
Foreign corporation	Form 355
Domestic corporation (part of a MA Combined group)	Form 355C
Foreign corporation (part of a MA Combined group)	Form 355C
Corporate trust	Form 3F
Domestic S corporation	Form 355S
Foreign S corporation	Form 355S

Corporations	State Form to File	Federal Form to File
Small domestic corporation	Form 355 SBC (small business corporation)	Form 1120
Domestic corporation	Form 355	Form 1120
Foreign corporation	Form 355	Form 1120
Domestic corporation (part of a MA Combined group)	Form 355C	Form 1120
Foreign corporation (part of a MA Combined group)	Form 355C	Form 1120
Quarterly estimated payments	See schedule above	See schedule above
Annual tax liability under $250,000 (state)	Form 355-ES (Annual tax liability over $1,000)	Form 8109 or EFTPS (consult IRS)

S Corporations	State Form to File	Federal Form to File
Domestic S corporation	Form 355S	Form 1120-S
Domestic corporation	Form 355	Form 1120
Foreign S corporation	Form 355S	Form 1120-S
Corporate trust	Form 3F	Form 1120 or 1120A, or other form (consult IRS)

The following table shows which return each type of shareholder should file:

Type of Shareholder	Form to File
Full-year resident individual	Form 1

Nonresident/part-year resident individual	Form 1-NR/PY
Trust or estate	Form 2
Domestic corporation	Form 355
Foreign corporation	Form 355
Domestic corporation (part of a MA Combined group)	Form 355C
Foreign corporation (part of a MA Combined group)	Form 355C
Corporate trust	Form 3F
Domestic S corporation	Form 355S
Foreign S corporation	Form 355S

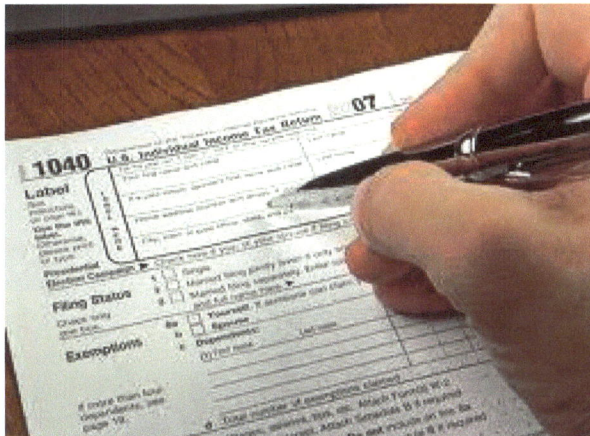

CHAPTER 8

PAYROLL TAXES

"There is no security on this earth, there is only opportunity."

- General Douglas MacArthur

PAYROLL TAXES

The IRS, Social Security Administration and most states require employers to make appropriate withholdings from employee wages. They also require that withholding be deposited and a proper accounting made of such amounts withheld. Failure to make necessary tax payments in time can subject you to penalties and interest as well as potential liens against your property. Employers are required to withhold from their employee's payroll the following items:

- Federal income tax.

- State income tax. (This is a state "trustee tax"; see State Trustee Taxes section above.)

- The employee's share of social security and Medicare taxes (FICA).

Additionally, employers are liable for the following taxes, which are related to or based upon payroll:

- Federal unemployment tax (FUTA).

- State unemployment insurance.

- The employer's share of social security and Medicare taxes (FICA).

New requirements exist for filing certain information returns on magnetic media to the IRS depending upon the type of form and number of forms to be filed. Substantial penalties exist for failure to file on magnetic media if such reporting is required.

New Hire Reporting Law

All employers, regardless of size or type of business, are required by law to report all newly hired employees, employees returning to work after 30 days, and independent contractors who will be earning $600 or more to the Massachusetts Department of Revenue (DOR) within 14 days of hire. This information is then compared to DOR's database of individuals who are required to pay child support. When there is a match, DOR notifies the employer to withhold child support and remit the funds to DOR for distribution to families entitled to support. The information is also used to combat fraud in programs run by various state and federal agencies. For further information contact

Agranovich Accounting and Payroll

1007 Chestnut St. Suite A

Newton, MA, 02464

Phone: (617)840-0982

lev@agstax.com

Employer Responsibility under Health Care Reform

Under Massachusetts' first-in-the-nation health care reform law, employers with 11 or more employees must make a "fair and reasonable" contribution to their full-time employees' health insurance costs. They are also required to establish a Section 125 Plan to allow all of their employees to pay their health insurance premiums on a pre-tax basis. By law, all Massachusetts adults must show that they have enrolled in a health insurance plan or lose their personal income tax deduction on their 2007 state taxes.

To learn more about employer responsibilities under the new law, contact

Agranovich Accounting and Payroll

Phone: (617)840-0982

lev@agstax.com

CHAPTER 9

INSURANCE

"Live as if you were to die tomorrow... Learn as if you were to live forever."

- Mahatma Gandhi

Unemployment Insurance

In general, if you have employees working one or more days in each of thirteen (13) weeks (need not be consecutive) during a calendar year, or if you pay wages of $1,500 or more in any calendar quarter, you are liable for contributions under the Massachusetts Unemployment Insurance Law. A new or successor business must notify the Massachusetts Division of Unemployment Assistance (DUA) immediately by registering their business with DUA to establish an Employer Account Number (EAN) and DUA QUEST ID. DUA QUEST is a self-service system that allows employers to register their business, and manage their unemployment insurance account and services online.

Employers pay two separate contributions to fund unemployment insurance. The federal contribution is paid to the IRS under the Federal Unemployment Tax Act (FUTA). The state contributions paid to DUA are deposited into the Massachusetts Unemployment Compensation Fund, and are used solely to pay benefits to eligible workers filing claims against Massachusetts firms.

Your state contribution is "experience rated." How much you pay depends on a variety of factors, including the size of your payroll, the number of employees, and amount of unemployment insurance benefits charged against your account, and the amount of reserves in your account and in the Massachusetts Unemployment Compensation Fund. For more information please contact the Agranovich Accounting and Payroll.

Federal Unemployment Insurance Tax (FUTA)

The Federal Unemployment Insurance Tax (FUTA) is currently 6.2% of wages paid during the year. The tax applies to the first $7,000 the employer pays each employee as wages during the calendar year. Generally, you can take a credit against your FUTA tax for amounts you paid into the state unemployment funds. This credit cannot be more than 5.4% of taxable wages. The employer is responsible for FUTA tax. The employer cannot deduct it from the employee's wages. Taxes are determined by federal Form 940. For questions on FUTA you can contact the Agranovich Accounting and Payroll.

Worker's Compensation Law

The Department of Industrial Accidents (DIA) is responsible for overseeing the Workers' Compensation system in Massachusetts. The department can help you if you are an employer in Massachusetts, an injured worker, an insurer, or an attorney. The Employers' Guide to the Massachusetts Workers' Compensation System has been compiled to assist employers to better understand the Massachusetts Workers' Compensation System. Included in this guide are sections on: who must be covered; what injuries must be reported; the reporting/claim process; reducing your insurance rate, and other questions and answers. To receive your copy, please contact The Agranovich Accounting and Payroll.

CHAPTER 10

SELECTING PROFESSIONAL ADVISORS

"Nothing great was ever achieved without enthusiasm."

- Ralph Waldo Emerson

SELECTING PROFESSIONAL ADVISORS

Professional advisors are the fundamentals to have success in your business. Your team of professional advisors should comprise a tax accountant, a lawyer and consultant knowledgeable and experienced in business ownership. They can assist you with ideas in areas which you have small experience. In order for your business to run efficiently, your business advisors will supplement their business ideas and knowledge.

Because of the costs associated with hiring an accountant or a lawyer, some business owners tend to attempt the do-it-yourself approach. But you might be putting your own business at risk on this. The right accountant, attorney and consultant are your best security; their expertise can help save you money which in turn can be used to increase profits.

You should be very selective in your screening process. The right selection will enhance your prospects for profit and growth; the wrong selection will be costly in terms of time, money and stress. The most common selection criteria include qualifications, experience, compatible personality, confidence and competence in the area concerned, and fees. Having a comparison of a least three advisors is the ideal approach before you select the one for your needs.

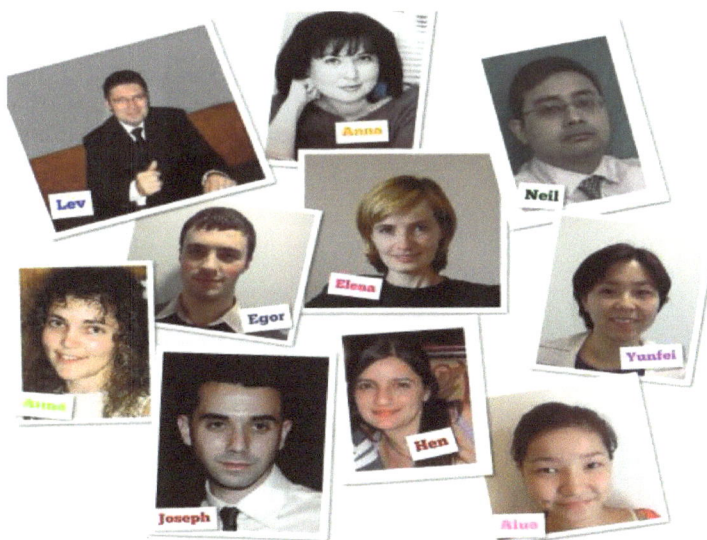

CONCLUSION

You now have a helpful kit or guide to begin with a business. In this kit, you could effectively handle any kind of problems that might come across in starting with a business. Just follow the step-by-step processes and tips in this starting a new business kit. A lot of successful businessmen were the images of a successful company with thorough planning. First, you have to have an appropriate legal entity to manage. Develop a business plan. This includes marketing strategies, financial forecast and the road map to start for a new business. Obtain a source of credit and finance for your business. This reflects the importance of a good business plan, it is the primary means utilized in acquiring financing. Once financing is attained, the business plan will also state a course of action. Always seek advices from professional advisors in areas which you are not sure of. Their expertise can help save you money which in turn can be used to increase profits. We desire for your success and welcome you to the world of free enterprise. Good luck!

www.ingramcontent.com/pod-product-compliance
Lightning Source LLC
Chambersburg PA
CBHW041451210326
41599CB00004B/209